GOING HOME TO NICODEMUS

The Story of an African American Frontier Town and the Pioneers Who Settled It

BY DANIEL CHU & BILL SHAW

JULIAN ⊗ MESSNER
Published by Silver Burdett Press
Morristown, New Jersey

Copyright © 1994 by Dan Chu and Associates

Book design by Rosemary Buonocore and Sylvia Frezzolini
Map on page 10 by Erik S. MacPeek

JULIAN MESSNER and colophon are trademarks
of Simon & Schuster.

10 9 8 7 6 5 4 3 2

Library of Congress Cataloging-in-Publication Data

Chu, Daniel   Going Home To Nicodemus / by Daniel Chu and Bill Shaw
    p. cm.
Includes bibliographical references and index.
1. Nicodemus (Kan.)—History. 2. Afro-Americans—
Kansas—Nicodemus—History.   I. Shaw, Bill, 1948- . II. Title
F689. N5C48 1994   94-27139
978.1'163—dc20   CIP
                AC
ISBN 0-671-88723-8 (hardcover)
ISBN 0-671-88722-X (paperback)

PHOTO CREDITS:
Dan Chu: pages 11, 12, 17, 75(right), 78, 85(left)
William K. Geiger: pages 4 and 88
The Granger Collection, New York: page 22
Green Bay Packers: page 75(left)
Kansas Collection, University of Kansas Libraries:
    pages 61(left and right), 63, 66
Kansas State Historical Society: pages 24, 26, 28, 32,
    33, 44, 53, 58, 62, 85
Kansas State University, Minorities Collection: pages 38 and 51
Barbara Laing/Black Star: pages 13, 14, 69, 71, 83
Manufactured in Mexico

 For Lenore

Nicodemus, Kansas as it is today.

The year was 1878, and Willianna Hickman found herself in a place she had never been before. Kansas was its name, and it was, Willianna had been told, the "Promised Land."

Willianna Hickman was thirty-one years old and a woman of color. This was one of the terms commonly used in the nineteenth century to describe an African American. Willianna and her husband, the Reverend Daniel Hickman, had traveled to Kansas from Georgetown, in north central Kentucky where the Reverend Hickman had been the minister of the Mount Olive Baptist Church.

All but the youngest in Daniel's Kentucky congregation had been born in slavery. But now, thirteen years after the end of the American Civil War, they were free men and women. No longer could they be bought and sold as property to be kept or disposed of at the whim of masters.

For all of that, however, America's leaders had not given enough thought as to what was to become of the four million freed slaves in the South. The freed men and women owned neither land nor homes and had little, if any, money. Most could not read or write. During slavery, they had toiled on southern plantations as field hands or household servants. They knew little else.

Now they were at liberty to leave the plantations and go wherever they wished. But where would that be? How were they to feed and house themselves? Where would they find work? How could people who had so little survive?

For the members of Reverend Hickman's church group, an answer came during the winter of 1877-1878. It came in the person of a white visitor named W.R. Hill.

W.R. Hill was a land promoter from Kansas, far away to the west. Hill told the Georgetown church members that there was government land available for homesteading on the western frontier. There was lots of it, and it was practically free for the asking. To claim a quarter section of land—160 acres—a homesteader had little more to do than show up.

Think of it! How could someone who had nothing, and no way of getting anything, turn down an offer like that?

The idea of homesteading became more attractive as Hill talked on. He and his partners had put together a special package for blacks only: a new town on the prairie run by blacks exclusively for blacks. Even as he spoke, W.R. Hill confided, hundreds of black settlers already were moving to this new community, a town that bore an intriguing name: Nicodemus.

To the Georgetown, Kentucky church audience on that wintry night, W.R. Hill's words were like an answered prayer. Here was a chance, the first for any of them, to own a piece of land, to be independent and self-supporting, to make their own way in life. It was a chance to leave behind the racial hostility and discrimination they had always known.

Out on the open plains of the Kansas frontier, W.R. Hill said, blacks and whites would live as equals.

With the coming of spring, about two hundred members of the Reverend Hickman's church packed up their few belongings and joined the great western migration. From the hills of Kentucky, they went off in two groups for Kansas and a new life.

The migrants from Kentucky reached Ellis in western Kansas by rail in just a few days. But an outbreak of measles among the children brought sudden tragedy. Some of them died, but Daniel and Willianna Hickman and their six children were among the luckier ones. They survived the outbreak. After a two-week delay in Ellis, the Hickmans and the other families hired horses and wagons for the final leg of their journey.

What a journey it was!

Guided by compass, they traveled two more days across roadless plains marked here and there by a few trees, deer trails, and buffalo wallows, or watering holes. At night the men built roaring campfires and fired their guns in the air to keep wild animals away. The women unpacked bedding and cooked a meal while the children slept or played games within the shadow of the fire's glow.

Worn from travel, Willianna Hickman was almost totally spent by the time her group arrived at its destination. She felt even worse when she got her first look at it.

Nicodemus was not the Promised Land she had expected, not what she had hoped for. To Willianna's dismay, there lay before her an entire community of people living in holes in the ground. The people were burrowed into the earth like the prairie dogs Willianna had seen on the trek from Ellis.

More than a half century later, when she was ninety, Willianna Hickman still vividly remembered her shock and astonishment on that spring day in 1878:

> When we got in sight of Nicodemus, the men shouted, "There is Nicodemus." Being very sick, I hailed this news with gladness. I looked with all the eyes I had. "Where is Nicodemus? I don't see it." My husband pointed out various smokes coming out of the ground and said, "That is Nicodemus." The families [there] lived in dugouts. . . . The scenery was not at all inviting, and I began to cry.
>
> —Topeka [Kansas] *Daily Capital*, 1937

To read the history books, you'd think only white people went West after the Civil War. But blacks also came out here and played an important role in the settling of the frontier. Nicodemus is an overlooked chapter in American history, and the beauty of it is, it still lives.

—Angela Bates, President of the Nicodemus Historical
Society, in a 1991 interview

Despite her crushing disappointment, Willianna Hickman, her family, and their fellow pioneers did not turn back. The rough conditions of life on the western frontier, in circumstances so lacking in comforts, stunned even those who had experienced the cruelties of slavery. The new hardships they faced were many, more than enough to discourage all but the bravest and strongest.

Most of the pioneers from Kentucky stayed. They coped and endured. They held to their hopes and dreams and kept their faith. And because they and their children did what they did, Nicodemus has survived as the oldest—and now the only remaining—all-black frontier town on the Great Plains.

The holes in the ground that greeted Willianna Hickman are long gone now, but Nicodemus is still there.

Where is there?

If you were to take a map of the United States (minus Alaska and Hawaii) and place a finger on what looks like the middle, you would be almost pointing directly at Nicodemus. The exact geographical center of the conterminous forty-eight states—the states that share borders—lies in the part of Kansas just a short distance from Nicodemus.

Despite its central location, Nicodemus remains isolated and well off the beaten track. Nowadays, with modern highways and motor vehicles, it is a bit easier to get there. Where the pioneers took the better part of a day or more to travel the thirty or so miles between Ellis and Nicodemus, a car can cover the distance in forty-five minutes.

Along the way, you now see neatly kept farms with their windmills and fields of wheat, alfalfa, or sorghum. But there remains horizon-to-horizon expanses of prairie grass (mainly of the buffalo and bluestem varieties) waving in the breeze.

Except for the telephone poles, power lines, and roadways (paved or dirt), the scenery is not so different from what the early pioneers saw more than a century ago.

Trees are still few on these high plains—cottonwood and willow grow along the bottom lands near creeks and rivers, and elm, hackberry, white oak, sycamore, and other kinds stand singly or in small clumps in the open fields.

People are about as scarce as trees, too. With an average of just four persons living on each square mile, it is easy to feel lonely around here.

Approaching Nicodemus from the east along U.S. Highway 24, just inside the Graham County line, the first thing that catches your eye is a 100-foot tower painted a

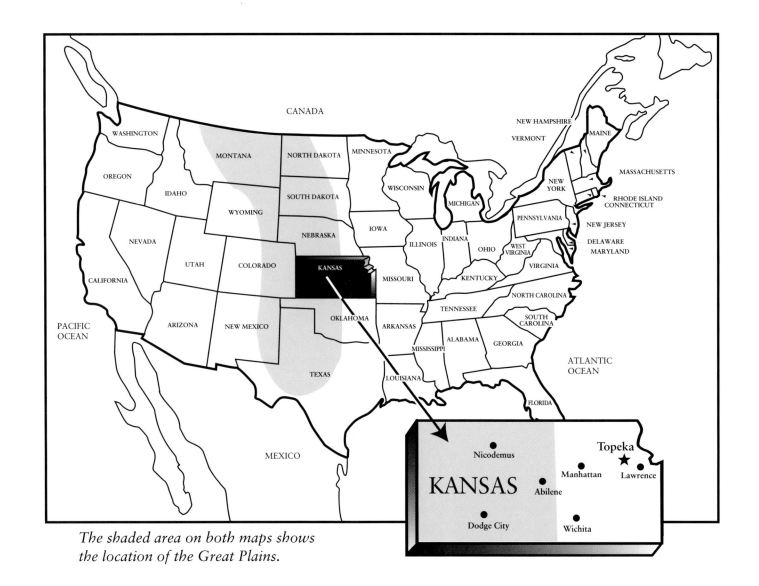

The shaded area on both maps shows
the location of the Great Plains.

Approaching Nicodemus on Highway 24.

robin's egg blue and shaped like a skinny pole. For a moment, you might wonder why there is a smokestack in a place with no industry except farming. On closer investigation, the polelike object turns out to be a water tower with the name of the town emblazoned in bold letters down its side.

A lighted roadside sign proclaiming that "NICODEMUS KANSAS WELCOMES YOU" confirms that you have found what you came for. So you pull off into a state-maintained rest area, a small park dotted with historical markers. One of them tells you that in 1976, the U.S. Department of the Interior designated Nicodemus a National Historical Landmark.

The First Baptist Church is an important part of community life. This structure, built in 1907, was replaced by a new building.

It is a quiet town. You can wander the streets and not see anyone. There are no traffic lights or stop signs, no stores or restaurants, no gas stations or public phones. Some of the older buildings, including an abandoned one-room schoolhouse, stand forlorn and crumbling. The eerie effect is that of an old movie set after the film crew has finished shooting and departed.

But Nicodemus is no ghost town. The townsite and its surrounding farms are still home to about fifty permanent residents. There are still a Baptist church filled with worshipers each Sunday, a town hall that serves as a community center, ten modest homes, and a modern ten-unit apartment complex for senior citizens.

And once a year, the last weekend in July or the first in August, Nicodemus comes alive. For a few days, the population of Nicodemus suddenly jumps tenfold or more. U.S.

Highway 24 becomes choked with cars bearing license plates from a dozen states as far away as California, Washington, or Virginia, or as close by as Nebraska, Colorado, or Oklahoma.

In cars, trailers, vans, and trucks, the geographically scattered children and grandchildren of Nicodemus make their way back home.

The occasion is the annual Emancipation Celebration observed every year—without fail—since 1878. In more recent times, most refer to it simply as "Homecoming," a

Emancipation Celebration. The crowds begin to assemble at the Nicodemus Township Hall.

giant family reunion in a town where nearly everyone is kinfolk or have been friends and neighbors for so long that they might as well be.

By the hundreds the now-dispersed members of the Nicodemus family return to renew their ties, to greet parents, brothers, sisters, aunts, uncles, and cousins, many not seen since last year. More likely than not, there will be a group of newborn children to be introduced to the clan for the first time.

Call it roots; call it what you want. They come home to remind themselves that this is where it all began and to reassure themselves that Nicodemus, in fact as in spirit, *is* still there.

Cousins Miranda Perfax (from California) and Angela Quick (from Colorado) exchange hugs.

This is a storybook place for us. Only the strong survive out here in the plains of Kansas. Turn back the pages of time, and you find people here with strong minds and hearts.

—Nicodemus-born Marvin Switzer, a trucking executive
in Kent, Washington, in a 1991 interview

The America of the mid-1800s was a very different place from what it is today. You may have to stretch your imagination to get a sense of what life was like back then.

In 1850 there were only 31 states and 23 million people (compared to 250 million now) in the United States. The population then was overwhelmingly rural; about 65 percent of the United States labor force, or nearly two of every three American workers, made their living off the land. Today, less than three percent of American workers are engaged in farming.

With the admission of California into the Union in 1850, the United States already was a nation that spanned a continent. In between those two ends, however, there remained a huge chunk of territory then regarded as a wilderness. This area included a vast stretch of grasslands in the very heart of the continent, a six-hundred-mile wide swath extending from Canada to Texas.

It's called the Great Plains.

Explorers of the region in the first part of the 1800s found the Great Plains "great" only in the sense that the area was large.

The army's Lieutenant Zebulon Pike (for whom Pikes Peak in Colorado was named) and Major Stephen H. Long (yes, a Colorado peak was named for him, too) passed separately through parts of the Great Plains. Both declared them to be wasteland. They described a region of sparse rainfall, almost treeless and featureless, most of it subject to withering heat in the summers and punishing blizzards in the winters.

Influenced by such dismal reports, the mapmakers of the times began to mark the area as the "Great American Desert."

Whatever it was or wasn't, the Great Plains stood as a gigantic obstacle, a test of body and spirit, for people moving westward across the continent. Fur trappers had to cross it to get to the Rocky Mountains and beyond to the Pacific Northwest. Prospectors and miners crossed it to reach new gold and silver strikes in Colorado and Nevada. Pioneering families bound for the Oregon Country crossed the ocean of grass in covered wagons (described by writers of the day as "prairie schooners"). The Mormons, fleeing religious persecution in the East, kept moving west until they reached the Utah Territory.

Few of the early pioneers, in fact, seriously considered settling on the barren, windswept plains. Since one measure of soil productivity was the number and size of trees that grew on the land, few thought that the prairie sod showed much promise as farm land. Zebulon Pike himself had declared that the prairies were best left to the Plains Indians who followed the migrating buffalo herds. That kind of white man's thinking served the Indians' interests for as long as it lasted.

The prairies near Nicodemus.

But all that changed during the second half of the 1800s. The westward surge of pioneers resumed full tilt after the Civil War. And the American frontier—the line separating the settled from the unsettled areas—crept westward with them.

Two developments provided the main thrusts for pushing western settlements onto the Great Plains. The first was the Homestead Act approved by Congress in 1862.

Under the Homestead Act, any male over twenty-one or a head of household could claim 160 acres of unoccupied public land by paying a modest filing fee. Homesteaders were required to live on and farm the land for five years, after which it was legally theirs.

The impact of the Homestead Act was dramatic. At a time when farming was still the main livelihood for Americans, the Act provided the basic resource needed to feed themselves and possibly earn a profit besides. As Frederick Jackson Turner, the famed historian of the American frontier, said, it was "the gift of capital."

A second key development was the railroad-building boom that came after the Civil War. The transcontinental railroad linking the West Coast with the East was completed in 1869. In between, regional rail lines spread over the central plains like an immense spider web.

Railroading was the biggest of big businesses in the Gilded Age, as the period after the Civil War is known. As with any business, it could get even bigger with an expanding customer base. Land-hungry pioneers could help to fill the seats and baggage cars of trains heading westward. And once they had settled and begun producing, they would ship the yields of their farms and ranches back to the rich markets of the East. Thus, the railroads had a direct interest in encouraging the peopling of the empty plains.

Railroad agents began touring the crowded cities and towns of the East and South to attract new settlers to the Great Plains. These agents crossed the Atlantic Ocean in search of potential new immigrants to America from Europe.

The concept of "Manifest Destiny" also helped attract settlers to the West. This was the idea that God intended the United States to be a single nation stretching from the Atlantic to the Pacific Oceans. Thus, it was not altogether surprising that the public's view of the Great Plains took a sudden turn for the better. Rather than the Great American Desert, the Great Plains were beginning to be seen as something more like an unspoiled garden spot, a place full of possibilities for those in search of a better life.

In reality, the Great Plains were never as bleak as some had said. But then, neither was the region as fertile as others claimed. Unreliable rainfall made the area prone to drought. And it was a place vulnerable to all sorts of natural disasters, including lightning-ignited wild fires, insect plagues, and tornadoes.

But by the mid-1800s, farming techniques had gotten better, too. One improvement were plows made of hardened steel that cut more easily into the tangle of grass roots just beneath the hard prairie surface. Another was the practice of "dry-land farming," in which land planted with crops one year was left fallow the next—the off year giving the land time to rebuild its moisture content. To this day, dry-land farming is still used successfully in the arid regions where irrigation is not possible or too expensive.

Finally, one other factor was behind the increasing numbers of homesteaders pushing onto the Great Plains in the 1870s. By then all of the regions to the east had been declared settled, their choicest lands already taken. Now, the Great Plains were where the frontier began. Land-hungry pioneers *had* to go there to seek their dreams.

In this vast state where [John] Brown has caused blood to flow in his righteous wrath, there was said to be land for all, and land especially for poor blacks who for so long had cherished the thought of a tiny patch of America that they could call their own.

—Historian Robert G. Athearn, In Search of Canaan: Black Migration to Kansas, 1879-80

As with white pioneers, free land and a chance to make a new start were the twin pulls that drew the black settlers to the open West. But in striving toward their new beginnings, blacks and whites hardly started on an equal footing.

To be sure, a sequence of amendments to the Constitution after the Civil War lifted the spirits of the freed men and women. The Thirteenth Amendment (1865) ended slavery. The Fourteenth (1868) secured their citizenship rights. The Fifteenth (1870) banned any abridgment to voting rights "on account of race, color, or previous conditions of servitude."

But in matters of day-to-day life, African Americans were hardly any better off than before. They might be free by law, but the bitter legacies of slavery still survived. As slaves they existed only to serve the needs of their owners. As freed men and women, they were on their own and had to learn to help themselves.

During the Reconstruction Era after the Civil War, the federal government made a well-intentioned attempt at meeting the immediate needs of the freed slaves. It set up the Freedmen's Bureau in 1865, to provide relief in the form of food, medicine, and jobs. More than one thousand schools were built throughout the South to educate African American children.

But the government programs were never adequate and did not begin to lay a foundation for bringing a long oppressed people into mainstream America. Even some well-meaning whites doubted that blacks could ever rise to a level of complete equality in American society. The outright bigots, notably members of the Ku Klux Klan, used violence and terror to maintain white supremacy.

Farming the land was what most plantation-born freedmen knew. Now they were farmers without land and with no real way of acquiring any. Some remained on or returned to the same plantations where they once were slaves, working under conditions that seemed little changed by emancipation. Others were forced into sharecropping, farming other people's land for a small portion of the harvest.

Many African Americans in the South had no work at all. Some with specialized skills, such as bricklaying or blacksmithing, found themselves shut out of the job market by whites-only guilds and unions.

When Reconstruction faltered—it ended entirely in 1877—racism returned unchecked to deny African Americans their civil rights. In the late 1800s, Southern legislatures began to pass a long series of humiliating "Jim Crow" laws. These began with the separation of whites and blacks on public transportation and were eventually extended to include schools, hospitals, theaters, hotels, and restaurants; to public waiting rooms, toilets, and even drinking fountains; to residential areas for the living and cemeteries for the dead. Racial segregation became the cornerstone of the southern way of life.

Artist Thomas Hart Benton captured the life of the black sharecropper in this painting called "Ploughing It Under."

Pioneers of all races headed for the frontier to escape from old ways of life that they disliked. Black pioneers had even more reason for seeking new homes in the West. And for tens of thousands of African Americans in the late 1800s, Kansas would be the destination of choice.

Why Kansas?

Because they had heard that was where the free land was. And because Kansas was where a fiery abolitionist named John Brown had first come to fame in the years before the Civil War.

Before Kansas became a state, Congress had left it up to the people living there to decide whether to permit or to ban slavery in the territory. The rivalry between anti-slavery Northerners and pro-slavery Southerners who flocked there soon turned it into a war zone known as "Bleeding Kansas."

New Englander John Brown was one of those who went to Kansas ready for battle. He was convinced that slavery was a sin and any means to abolish it would be justified. When pro-slavery men sacked the abolitionist stronghold of Lawrence, Kansas, in 1856, John Brown took it upon himself to exact ruthless revenge. His armed followers attacked a settlement of Southerners and brutally killed five pro-slavery men.

Ultimately, the slavery issue in Kansas was settled not through bloodshed but because the abolitionists outnumbered and outlasted their opponents. Kansas entered the Union as a free state in 1861.

By then John Brown had created even more notice elsewhere. In a failed attempt in 1859 to spark a slave rebellion all over the South, he and a small band of his followers seized the federal arsenal at Harpers Ferry, Virginia (now in West Virginia). Brown was wounded, captured, and tried for treason. He was convicted and hanged.

John Brown believed he had a divine mission to make sure Kansas entered the Union as a free state. John Steuart Curry's mural of a fiery Brown is in the Kansas State Capitol at Topeka.

Southern whites feared and loathed John Brown as a murdering terrorist. But the black slaves of the South saw him as a hero, a martyr who sacrificed his own life in the fight to free others. For years thereafter, John Brown's historical link to Kansas gave it a reputation as a place friendly to black people and as the freest of all the states.

Among the first to test that idea was another man of vision. But this man was an African American, and his methods were entirely peaceful.

His name was Benjamin Singleton who was better known, he said, as "Old Pap."

Once a slave, Pap Singleton escaped slavery and became a skilled carpenter. He returned to his native Tennessee after the Emancipation Proclamation (1863). Unhappy with the conditions he found there, Pap Singleton came up with the idea of setting up black communities in the West that would be separate but coexist with the surrounding white communities.

In 1873 Pap Singleton led a group of about 300 black settlers to Cherokee County in the southeastern corner of Kansas. His trailblazing effort attracted newspaper publicity and made Pap famous as a kind of latter-day Moses leading his people into the "Promised Land."

Through circulars and advertisements, Singleton praised Kansas as the place to relocate to for southern blacks. In 1879 thousands of poor blacks—at least 20,000, possibly as many as 40,000—caught Pap's "Kansas fever." By rail, by steamboat up the Mississippi and Missouri Rivers, on wagons, mules, or on foot, they fled the South for Kansas.

It was a haphazard exodus, unplanned and disorganized. Most "Exodusters," as they came to be called, were desperately poor, illiterate, and had few skills. Lacking the will or means to take on the hard business of homesteading on the frontier, few ventured onto the high plains of western Kansas. Instead, most clustered in the cities and towns of eastern Kansas, surviving however they could.

At first, Kansans welcomed the Exodusters. They soon changed their minds, however. The newcomers had arrived so suddenly and in such huge numbers that the local cities and towns were unable to provide much relief. From Kansas Governor John Pierce St. John on down, a new message went out to the poor African Americans in the South: Don't come to Kansas.

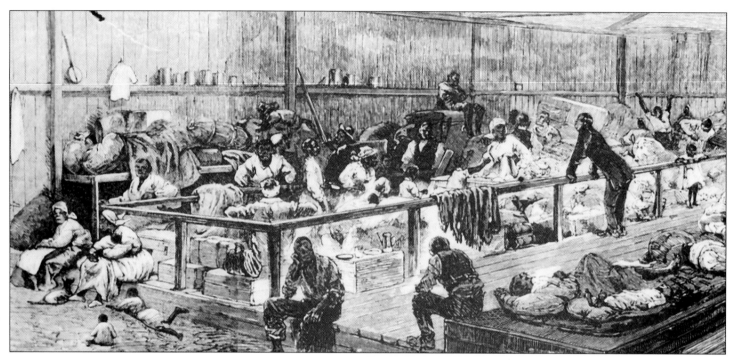

Exodusters waiting in Topeka. Some newcomers chose to remain in the towns and cities of eastern Kansas while others set out for the high plains of the western part of the state.

The Exodusters stopped coming the next year. And of those already in Kansas, roughly two-thirds soon left the state. Some died, some returned to the South. Many more moved to other places to pursue their dreams. As they departed, their towns and farm settlements shrank, then disappeared.

The one exception was a town called Nicodemus.

All colored people that want to go to Kansas on September 5th, 1877, can do so for $5.
—A handbill issued by the Nicodemus Town Company

Strictly speaking, the first settlers of Nicodemus were not Exodusters. Perhaps the town's founders knew of Pap Singleton, but there was no evidence they ever met him or had any dealings with him. Besides, Nicodemus was founded a full two years before the Exoduster surge began.

Still, it was the same desire for an all-black haven in the West that created Nicodemus.

The story of Nicodemus started with a black minister named W.H. Smith. He and a companion arrived in western Kansas sometime in the mid-1870s to scout out the place on behalf of friends back in Tennessee. In the course of their mission, Smith became acquainted with William R. Hill.

The Indiana-born Hill had emigrated to Kansas as a young man and took up an occupation that was peculiar to that time and place. He was a homestead locator and town developer, a kind of frontier real estate broker.

Under the law, private groups could organize town companies that would claim a portion of government-owned land to set up a townsite. Once a town had been organized into lots, the developers could turn around and sell the lots at a profit to individual buyers. The town companies took care of arrangements and completed the paperwork—for a fee.

W.H. Smith and W.R. Hill took the lead in forming two land companies. The first was the Nicodemus Town Company, organized from the beginning as an all-black community. The other was the Hill City Town Company that was to be an all-white counterpart of Nicodemus.

The interlocking nature of the two companies was revealed in the roles Smith and Hill gave themselves. In the Nicodemus Company, Smith served as president with Hill as treasurer. In the Hill City Company, they reversed their titles: Hill was president and Smith the treasurer.

Land promoter W.R. Hill played a leading role in the founding of the Nicodemus colony.

In addition to Smith and Hill, the Nicodemus Company had five other partners, all of them African American men who hailed from Kentucky. Little is known about most of the original black directors except for the Reverend Simon P. Roundtree. He was said to have been branded on his cheek, a cruel punishment for his audacity in learning to read and write while he was a slave. As the only literate person among the black originators of Nicodemus, the Reverend Roundtree served as company secretary.

The most experienced land promoters among them, W.R. Hill, chose the Nicodemus townsite. One account told of how he spent an afternoon walking barefoot around the prairies near the south branch of the Solomon River. Exhausted, he laid down to rest out in the open. Awakened by the sun the next morning, Hill decided on the spot that this was the place for Nicodemus.

But no one knows for sure how the town's name was chosen. Unlike W.R. Hill, who named Hill City after himself, W.H. Smith showed modesty in not calling his town "Smith City."

Instead, the company directors chose a name filled with symbolism, an inspired choice that tied the town's name to the idea of black freedom.

This particular Nicodemus was a legendary figure familiar in song and verse to slaves who had worked the southern plantations. He was said to have been an African prince brought in chains to the New World during colonial times and was reputedly the first slave to buy his freedom. He also predicted that white people would one day pay a heavy price for enslaving black people.

So that no one should miss the link between legend and town, the promoters borrowed from an original song titled "Wake Nicodemus", changed some of the words around to suit their own purposes, and then added it to their sales literature, much in the way TV commercials today often use catchy jingles to sell a product. This version of the Nicodemus song went:

> Nicodemus was a slave of African birth,
> And was bought for a bagful of gold;
> He was reckoned a part of the salt of the earth.
> But he died years ago, very old.
>
> Nicodemus was a prophet, at least he was as wise,
> For he told of the battles to come;
> How we trembled with fear, when he rolled up his eyes,
> And we heeded the shake of his thumb.
>
> (The chorus):
> Good times coming, good times coming,
> Long, long time on the way;
> Run and tell Elijah to hurry up Pomp,
> To meet us under the cottonwood tree,
> In the Great Solomon Valley
> At the first break of day.

The directors of the Nicodemus Town Company thought big. Their ambition was to build "the largest colored colony in America." Nothing less would do.

The whole of Nicodemus Township occupied more than thirty sections of 640 acres each, totaling more than 19,200 acres altogether. In June of 1877, the Town Company filed a claim for 160 acres of that space—a quarter section—in the southeastern corner of the township on which to build the town of Nicodemus.

While the rest of the township would remain open farmland available for homesteading, the town would serve as the social and commercial focus for the entire settlement.

Town streets that ran in a north and south direction were simply called "First," "Second," "Third," and so on to "Seventh." But with a patriotic flourish, the streets running east and west were to be named "Washington," "Adams," "Jefferson," "Madison," "Monroe," and "Jackson," after the first American presidents. The one exception was the east-west street farthest north, which, for reasons unclear, was called "South Street."

For its help in locating a homestead and filing the necessary papers, the town company charged fees ranging from $2 to $30. For those who wished to start a business within the townsite or to live there, or both, the going price of residential lots was $5 each and $75 for a commercial lot.

With its price list set, all that the Nicodemus Town Company needed now was customers. An early advertising handbill printed by the company was addressed specifically "To the Colored Citizens of the United States." Other circulars emphasized that a black

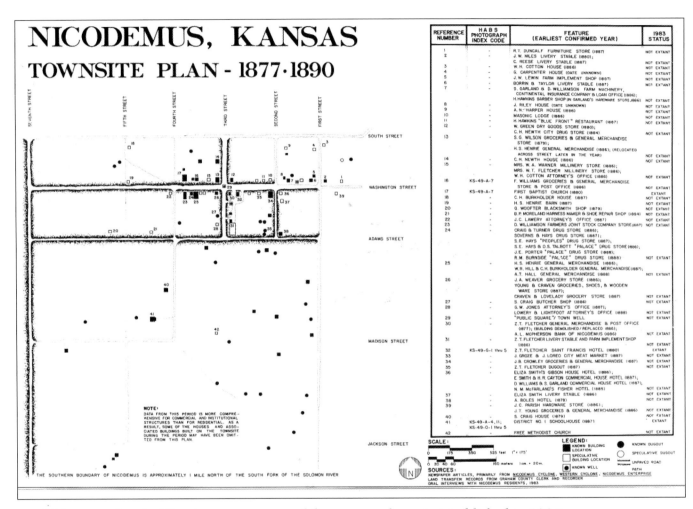

This map of early Nicodemus was created for a research project published in 1986.

man was president of the Nicodemus Town Company; that six of its seven directors were black, that the town they were planning would be exclusively for black colonists.

"We are proud to say it is the finest country we ever saw," one handbill said boldly. "The soil is of a rich, black, sandy loam. The country is rather rolling, and looks most pleasing to the human eye. The south fork of the Solomon River flows through Graham County. . . and has an abundance of excellent water, while there are numerous springs of water abounding throughout the Valley. . . . There is also some timber; plenty for fire use, while we have no fear [that] we will find plenty of coal."

One problem with sending out printed handbills was that most freed blacks, for whom the leaflets were intended, could not read. So the Nicodemus promoters—Smith, Hill, and Roundtree—took to the road to recruit settlers for Nicodemus.

Speaking to black church groups in Kentucky, W.R. Hill was especially eloquent. Oh yes, he assured his listeners, there

This was one of the first circulars issued by the town company to attract settlers.

THE LARGEST COLORED COLONY IN AMERICA!

Is now locating in the Great Solomon Valley, in Graham County, two hundred and forty miles north west of Topeka.

Mr. Smith, the President of the Colony, is a colored man and has lived for the last three years in the Solomon Valley.

All letters of inquiry regarding Soil, Climate, and Locations, should be addressed to W. H. SMITH, or his Secretary, S. P. ROUNDTREE, Topeka, Kansas, until May 15th, 1877; then at Ellis, Ellis Co., Kan. A Postoffice will be located in June at

NICODEMUS,

which is beautifully located on the north side of the south fork of the Solomon River, near the line of Graham and Rooks Counties, 14 miles east of Hill City, and is designed for the Colored Colony. By September 1st the Colony will have houses erected and all branches of mercantile business will be opened out for the benefit of the Colony. A Church edifice and other public buildings will be erected. No Saloons or other houses of ill-fame will be allowed on the town site within five years from the date of this organization.

We invite our colored friends of the Nation to come and join with us in this beautiful Promise Land.

Dated at Topeka, Kansas, April 16, 1877.

TRUSTEES:

WM. EDMONS,   JEFF. LENZE,   JERRY ALLSAPP.
W. H. SMITH,   -   -   -   President.
BERY CARR,   -   -   -   Vice President.
SIMON P. ROUNDTREE,   -   Secretary.

W. R. HILL, Treasurer and Gen'l Manager.

NOTE.—This Colony has made special arrangements for provisions for the Summer season. For Emigrant and Freight Rates, address our Treasurer,

W. R. HILL,
(BOX 120.)   NORTH TOPEKA, KANSAS.

was plenty of animals out there on the high plains that could be hunted for food. And there was a herd of wild horses that pastured nearby that could be caught, tamed, and trained to pull plows and wagons.

Later it turned out that many of Hill's promises would prove false, raising a raft of questions that would be argued for years.

Were the Nicodemus promoters a smooth-talking band of liars? Or were they just poor planners? Did they undertake their Nicodemus project to create a haven for a people sorely in need of one? Or were they mostly interested in turning a fast profit?

Much of the debate revolved around the character of W.R. Hill.

One prominent Nicodemus leader from the early days, a lawyer named W.L. Sayers, told local historian William J. Belleau that Hill was "very good to the colored man and worked continually in their interests."

But some of Hill's white rivals in Graham County saw him differently. One critic said Hill and his partners "cared no more for the welfare of the colored man than they did for the smallest insect that crawls."

Whichever the case, it was clear that W.R. Hill was better at recruiting settlers for Nicodemus than in caring for their needs. "By September 1st," a handbill he signed in 1877 stated, "the Colony will have houses erected and all branches of mercantile business will be opened out for the benefit of the Colony. A Church edifice and other public buildings will be erected. . . ."

September 1st arrived, and there were no houses, no buildings, no businesses. No wells had been sunk, no supplies laid in, no streets laid out.

There was nothing in Nicodemus except thirty African American pioneers wondering how they would survive in the wilderness of the Great Plains.

My grandad and grandma got here in Nicodemus and stayed. They used to go from here to Ellis in wagons to get groceries. They stay'd there all night and come back the next morning. They said the wolves were real bad along the way. They'd have meat in the wagons, and they'd get up there and beat the wolves off, knocked 'em on the head with clubs and things.

—Nicodemus farmer Don Moore, in a 1993 interview

Most of the first pioneers to arrive in Nicodemus came in five separate groups. The members of each group already knew one another, whether as relatives, friends, or members of the same church. And because they had bonded in some way beforehand and understood the need to pull together, they formed the solid core that saw Nicodemus through its first trying days and years.

W.R. Hill himself guided the first group of thirty settlers to the townsite on July 30, 1877. He brought them in from Topeka, the state capital 240 miles to the east, where the group had been organized by Hill, Roundtree and Z. (Zach) T. Fletcher.

Jenny Fletcher, Zach's wife, was the only woman in Nicodemus during the first month. She and Zach's brother, T. (Thomas) J. Fletcher, would be bulwarks of strength when the going was the toughest.

It took no time at all for the first arrivals to realize that their Promised Land was not very promising. Many felt cheated and began to talk openly of hanging W.R. Hill.

Hill decided that his wisest move at that moment would be to hide. He sought out the home of a white friend for refuge. Later he was concealed in a wagon load of hay and smuggled to the town of Stockton twenty miles to the east. W.R. Hill stayed in Stockton until the anger in Nicodemus subsided.

In September 1877 a second group of 130 families, numbering about 300 people, reached Nicodemus, this time from Lexington, Kentucky. Many of them took one look at the empty prairie and were not happy with what they saw. The very next day, sixty of the families turned around and headed back east.

Those who did stay soon realized that they had come to Nicodemus too late in the growing season. There would be no harvest the first year. Their problem was compounded by the fact that the town promoters had not bought any supplies to tide the community over the first winter. And the nearest grocery store was at the railhead at Ellis, a walk of more than thirty miles each way.

But hadn't W.R. Hill told them that there was an abundance of wild game that could be hunted for food?

Yes, he had. But by this time, the game animals that might have been turned into meat for the table had migrated elsewhere in their own search for winter pasture.

With the onset of colder days and nights, shelter became a pressing need. At first the pioneers of Nicodemus huddled under makeshift lean-tos. But the relentless prairie winds blew the rickety structures to shreds.

Build cabins? The scarcity of timber made that impossible. Buy lumber? Even if they had the money—and most did not—there was not a commercial lumber mill close by.

So the Nicodemus pioneers did what they had to do. They burrowed into the ground. They built dugouts.

A dugout was just what it sounded like: a hole in the ground usually dug into the side of a small hill. Wielding hand tools such as picks, spades, or hoes, dugout builders excavated a rectangular space maybe fifteen or so feet long, fourteen feet wide, and about six feet deep. Because the terrain is slightly sloped, some of the dugout would be above ground. That part was enclosed by "bricks" made from the prairie sod itself.

The method for roofing a dugout was to lay willow saplings, tree branches, and prairie brush across a long ridge pole. Then a layer of dirt was piled and packed on top.

Entry to a dugout was through a door at one end with steps leading down to the dirt floor. A fireplace and chimney took up most of the other end.

Dugouts were unpleasant to live in. They were as dark, cramped, and stuffy as small caves. But they provided a shelter from the weather, and they could be built cheaply and quickly, especially if neighbors pitched in to help.

Which was exactly how the Nicodemus settlers built their first dugout. They had to hurry, for one of them, Mrs. Emily Williams, the wife of Charles Williams, was about to give birth.

Inside that dugout on October 30, 1877, Emily Williams gave birth to a son. Henry Williams was the first baby born in Nicodemus, Kansas.

Huddled in their dugouts, the Nicodemus settlers, including the infant, Henry Williams, endured that first winter. Sympathetic whites in nearby communities helped out with food. Help also came from Indians who were passing through.

These were the Osage Indians, a settled tribe in eastern Kansas, whose annual hunts took them into the Rocky Mountains. On their return trip, the Osage saw the plight of the Nicodemus pioneers. In the spirit of compassion and generosity that could often be found on the frontier, the Osage shared their meat supply with the hungry blacks.

Henry Williams (rear, center), seen with his family, was the first child born in Nicodemus.

The new Nicodemites soon absorbed the lessons of survival on the high plains. Jackrabbits could be snared, for example, and turned into a main dish. Sunflower stalks, willow twigs, and even dried animal dung—called "chips," as in "buffalo chips"—could be collected and burned as fuel for cooking and heating.

The smoke rising out of the ground from their fires was what Willianna Hickman saw when the next wave of settlers reached Nicodemus the following spring.

When I was growing up, there were still those dugouts and sod houses all over the prairie. My grandparents thought that living in a hole in the ground was all right because it was a whole lot better than being in those places where they were slaves.

—Nicodemus-born Versella Bates, in a 1993 interview

Two separate groups, both from Georgetown, Kentucky, and each headed by a Baptist minister, reached Nicodemus in the spring of 1878. This welcomed reinforcement boosted the population there for a time to more than six hundred.

The newest arrivals came in time for the spring planting, but they were not much better equipped for turning prairie into farmland than those already there. Most owned only the simplest farm tools.

Of the few horses that the first settlers brought with them from Topeka, only three survived the first winter. And the idea that wild horses in the area could be caught and harnessed to the plow turned out to be another of the town promoters' dreams. No one in Nicodemus ever caught a wild horse.

That left most Nicodemites with no other way to break the tough prairie sod except by hand. But if they had to swing an ax to punch holes in the unyielding ground to plant the seeds, that was just what they would do. And they did.

Tales of their grit and tenacity are still told and passed down from one generation to the next. There was the epic effort of one Nicodemus pioneer who, with just a hoe, single-handedly dug a four-foot-wide boundary trench around his quarter section. Another story told of a husband and wife who hitched their plow to the only animal they owned—a milk cow—and broke twelve acres of prairie sod to put in a first corn crop.

Through backbreaking labor and by making do, some settlers managed to cultivate as much as twenty acres. Others scraped by with what they could grow on only an acre or two. The average was about eight acres.

Nearly everyone in Nicodemus had to find a way to supplement his or her income. One of the more unusual ways was the scavenging of buffalo bones. By this time, buffalo hunters from the east had already cut a wanton swath through the high plains, slaughtering the herds wholesale and leaving the prairies strewn with buffalo carcasses rotting in the sun.

Then someone discovered that the buffalo bones had value. They could be collected and shipped back east by rail to be ground up and converted into fertilizer.

Before long, the gathering of buffalo bones became a Nicodemus enterprise involving entire families, including children. Wagon loads of bones were collected and hauled to a railhead where they were sold at a price of $6 to $8 a ton. This went on for a couple of years until the prairies were picked clean.

Another way to earn extra income was to find temporary work after the harvest. The men of Nicodemus hired themselves out for odd jobs in other frontier communities or worked as section hands repairing a stretch of track for the railroads. None of those jobs were close by, so the men walked hundreds of miles to eastern Kansas or out west to Colorado. They were away from home for days, weeks, sometimes months.

Meanwhile, the women and children of Nicodemus stayed behind to protect and maintain the precious family land from claim jumpers. They survived as best they could on short rations of boiled or fried rice until their men came home.

We went away a while last fall
A month or so, and that was all;
We earned enough to last us through,
Up to this time we've made it do.

Oh, Kansas Sun, Hot Kansas Sun!
As to the highest bluff we run,
And look away across the plain,
And wonder if it ne'er would rain....

—Anonymous Nicodemus poet quoted
in the Kansas City *Star*, 1905

The first two years in Nicodemus were so tough that most of the Nicodemus settlers had to turn to charity to meet some of their daily needs. Despite appeals to the Kansas governor, however, no relief ever came from the state government.

The town leaders had better success with private sources. Some white communities donated food and supplies. Private charities in eastern Kansas also helped. In one instance, the town company secretary, S.P. Roundtree, journeyed all the way to the Michigan State Fair, where he so moved his audience with a request for aid that several boxcar loads of supplies were sent to Nicodemus.

By the second spring, however, the situation in Nicodemus had much improved. A number of young and able new leaders took over the affairs of the town. And the fifth and last of the groups, a contingent of fifty settlers from Mississippi, reached Nicodemus in February 1879. The latest arrivals came well-equipped with teams of horses, farm tools, and supplies, and these they shared with the whole community.

It looked as if the Nicodemus settlement was going to make it after all. Amid this new optimism, the settlers began to reexamine their dependence on outside help. It seemed to most of them that charity from strangers did not keep with their wish for a self-sufficient community. Some also feared that taking charity only encouraged laziness among those who took it.

In April 1879, the Nicodemus settlers voted overwhelmingly to end all appeals for help from strangers. They also voted the Nicodemus Town Company out of existence.

From this time on, the success or failure of Nicodemus would rest entirely on what the community could do for itself.

ith the return of warmer days, Nicodemus literally began to take shape. One by one, the dugouts were replaced by new and improved dirt structures that were mostly or entirely above ground.

Just two years after the arrival of the first Nicodemus pioneers, the townspeople could already count thirty-five dwellings, two churches, two livery stables, a real estate office, a general store with a post office, and a hotel that was more like a boarding house.

Here and there, buildings made of locally quarried limestone—the cut blocks dragged or carted to the site—were rising. But most of the new structures were still constructed from that classic building material of the plains—the prairie sod.

To build a sod house, settlers began by cutting out strips of the prairie sod about two feet long, a foot wide, and three or four inches deep. These strips remained intact and did not crumble, because densely tangled grass roots knitted them together in a mat.

Next, the strips, grass-side down, were laid to build the walls. A second sod strip, placed parallel to the first, was put down to create a double thick wall. Then "bonding strips" were placed crosswise between each long layer to hold everything together.

As the walls rose, openings for a wooden door and windows were framed with lumber. With luck some settlers might even have had glass for the windows.

The roof of sod houses differed little from those found on dugouts. A long ridge pole held up rafters made of saplings, twigs, brush, and grass, topped by a layer of matted sod and then another of earth.

To finish the inside, the walls were plastered with a kind of powdered limestone mixed with sand and water. The floor was often bare earth, to which water and salt was applied to pack it more firmly.

At the beginning, homebuilt beds, tables, and chairs made from timber had to do. As conditions improved, they could be replaced with factory-made furniture. Washing and toilet facilities were always outdoors.

Sod houses were a step up from dugouts because windows could be installed for air and light. Above-ground construction also opened up possibilities of larger buildings without the need to dig gigantic holes.

The sod houses built by the first Nicodemus settlers were replaced by limestone houses such as the one shown here. Later, townspeople built wooden structures.

But "soddies" also shared certain drawbacks. They were hard to keep clean because bits and pieces kept falling off the walls and ceiling. And when it rained, you could count on a leaky roof that kept on dripping long after the storm passed. Occasionally, the whole waterlogged structure collapsed.

Another big problem with sod houses was that lots of crawling creatures—mostly bugs—came with the building material. Small rodents found it easy to burrow their way inside. Snakes—including poisonous prairie rattlesnakes in pursuit of small prey—sometimes made themselves at home in the thicket that was the roof. Stories were told of prairie settlers rigging canopies above their beds to prevent such unwanted guests from plopping on them in the middle of the night.

Not so dangerous, but no less bothersome, were the fleas that infested the grasslands. To fleas, a sod house was an extension of the plains with the dirt rearranged, and no amount of wetting and sweeping could keep them out. As a result, people who lived in soddies scratched a lot. They called it the "Kansas itch."

Soddies were not built to last, and not one sod house remains in Nicodemus today. Still, the town's oldest residents can remember growing up in them, and what they remember wasn't all bad.

Humble though they were, the classic sod houses did have virtues. Their earthworks served as excellent insulation, making soddies comfortably cool under the summer sun and surprisingly cozy when winter winds howled. Soddies were almost completely fireproof, an important consideration on a terrain swept periodically by fast-traveling grass fires. No one ever needed a bank mortgage on a sod house, so no one ever lost one to foreclosure.

For the Nicodemus pioneers—many of whom were slaves barely a dozen years earlier—the sod houses represented something more. For the first time in their lives, the people of Nicodemus were home owners, not mere tenants. No one could come along and order them out of their homes or shift them around at whim. That in itself was a meaningful step toward a freer, more secure life.

The lack of fancy housing did not keep the Nicodemus settlers from getting on with the task of building a community. In their rough sod houses, they organized their first churches, founded their first schools, and opened their first shops.

Most of the colonizing groups were led by preachers, so a pattern of regular worship was quickly reestablished on the Kansas frontier. At the start, Sunday services had to be held in the dugout of one or another of the members. But by 1879, the Reverend Daniel Hickman's Baptist group was well established at Mount Olive, one of three communities that sprang up within a few miles of the Nicodemus townsite. There they put up the first proper church in Nicodemus Township, a sod structure large enough to accommodate fifty worshipers at a time.

Two more churches soon went up within the townsite itself. One was a sod church called St. Paul's, build by a Methodist congregation that began with just five members. The other housed the Baptist group of the Reverend Silas M. Lee.

Education ranked almost as high on the Nicodemus settlers' scale of values. The literacy rate among the African American pioneers was lower than that of the whites around them. Yet it was surprisingly high for a people who so recently emerged from slavery. A census in 1880 found that more than one-third of the adults in Nicodemus could read, and one in four could write. Among the men, about half could do both. One of them, William Kirtley, had come to Nicodemus from Kentucky with a personal library of nearly a dozen books, including two Bibles and a copy of *Webster's Unabridged Dictionary*.

Making the most of what they had, the Nicodemites established Graham County's first school district in 1879. The first school, with fifteen pupils, met at Z.T. Fletcher's sod hotel. Jenny Fletcher was the town's first schoolteacher.

The school year had to be short because children, even younger ones, were expected to help with farm chores. So the terms ordinarily ran during the three or four months between crop-growing seasons. The lessons taught went beyond the basics of reading, writing, and arithmetic to include lessons in moral values and personal hygiene.

Zach Fletcher also was responsible for launching the town's first business, a general store. When his dugout emporium opened during the first winter, hardly anyone in Nicodemus had any money. That was probably just as well because Zach's store did not have much to sell beyond a small stock of cornmeal and syrup. His was a general store, said a local jokester, that was "generally out of everything."

In addition Fletcher was appointed Nicodemus's first postmaster, making him one of the first African Americans in the United States to head a post office. Zach took on the job, though, not to make history or money since the job paid next to nothing. Worse, he had to walk all the way to Ellis to get the mail. To make it worth his while, Fletcher waited until he figured enough of the mail had piled up at Ellis before walking there to bring it back.

Fans of Hollywood movie westerns know that when ranchers and farmers crossed paths, trouble often followed.

Ranchers needed large grazing areas for their herds to roam. The cattlemen thus resented farmers with their barbed wire fences closing off the open range and blocking easy access to precious watering holes. The farmers, for their part, did not take kindly to ranchers who drove their herds through the planted fields, trampling crops into dust.

Cattle ranchers had free run of the grasslands of western Kansas when the Nicodemus settlers arrived on the scene. On several occasions, the cattlemen deliberately set grass fires in an attempt to scare off the newcomers. Another time, cowboys rustled some livestock owned by the Nicodemus settlers, who, in this instance, fought back. They got hold of one of the offenders and held him hostage until the stolen animals were returned.

It happened that these quarrels in Nicodemus pitted whites against blacks, but race was not necessarily at the root of the conflict. White cowboys and white sodbusters fought each other just as bitterly in most parts of the West and for all the same reasons.

In contrast, white farmers on the Kansas frontier got on rather easily with the Nicodemus settlers during those early times. In a place where nearly everyone was in need, lending a hand just seemed like the most natural thing to do.

Westbound wagon trains of white pioneers regularly stopped off in Nicodemus to rest and resupply. While the blacks there had little enough to spare, they shared what they had. In exchange, the white settlers loaned their draft animals and tools to help the black farmers break the land for cultivation.

The early encounters between whites and blacks went off so well that a trickle of white businessmen, sensing the commercial potentials of Nicodemus, settled in to stay. Two of the most prominent among them were New York-born Samuel G. Wilson and William Green, from Rhode Island. They both opened general stores housed in large new stone buildings two stories tall.

Another white newcomer was C.H. Newth, an English immigrant who, at twenty-three, was already a practicing physician. Newth married a local white woman and settled on a nearby homestead. But he did most of his doctoring from his drugstore in town, where he attended to all cases, "promptly, day or night."

To have a resident doctor was quite an accomplishment for *any* frontier community. Yet the presence of Dr. Newth and the white businessmen changed Nicodemus from a self-segregated, all-black community to an integrated one in which African Americans predominated. That was not in keeping with the original plan for the town. But if anyone was troubled by the change, no one made a public fuss.

Quite the opposite, blacks and whites in Nicodemus worked together in a spirit of accommodation. Through unspoken understandings, they found ways to share political power.

An 1880 census listed 258 blacks and 58 whites as residents of Nicodemus Township. Owing to the black majority, almost all of the elective posts in the township, from trustees to justices of the peace, were filled by African Americans. One exception was the District 1 school board where there were two black members and one white.

Countywide, however, whites numbered nearly 3,800 to fewer than 500 blacks. But even as a minority within the county, blacks won at least a proportion of the elective posts. The leadership qualities of the Reverend Daniel Hickman, for example, so impressed all voters that he was elected a county commissioner. And in those early times, no one in all of Graham County commanded more respect than E. (Edward) P. McCabe.

Handsome, forthright, and well traveled, McCabe was born a free black in Troy, New York, in 1850, and educated in New England public schools. In time he turned up in New York City where he was employed as a clerk on Wall Street. Later, McCabe moved to Chicago, married a seamstress, and became the first black man to clerk at the Cook County treasurer's office.

In Chicago McCabe befriended Abraham T. Hall, a black newspaper editor. Together they went off to seek new opportunities on the frontier. Arriving in Nicodemus in April of 1878, McCabe and Hall became business partners, first in buying a sod hotel and then in opening a land office. And with all the confidence and energy of their youth, they launched themselves into the political life of their community.

Graham County's government was undergoing formal organization then, and Kansas Governor St. John tapped McCabe to serve as temporary county clerk while Hall was given the job of census taker. McCabe, in particular, soon came to wider notice. At the 1882 Republican Party Convention in Topeka, Kansas, attended by 394 white delegates and 6 black delegates, he was nominated as candidate for Kansas State Auditor (a post overseeing the state's finances). When he was elected easily a few weeks later, E.P. McCabe became the highest ranking black official of his time in the American West.

He left Nicodemus that year to take up his duties in Topeka. Two years later, he won a second term but then did not seek a third. Instead McCabe left Kansas, eventually

In the 1880s, E.P. McCabe was the highest-ranking African-American official in the West.

resurfacing in Oklahoma. There, in a replay of his Kansas career, McCabe served ten years as state auditor. He also took the lead in promoting Langston City and Liberty, two Oklahoma communities that, like Nicodemus, were intended as all-black towns.

McCabe's last years were full of disappointments and sorrow. When Oklahoma became a state in 1907, the Republicans lost control of the legislature, and McCabe lost his job. One of his daughters died that year, and another lay dying in a Chicago hospital. McCabe closed out his business in Oklahoma and returned to Chicago to be near her. He soon fell ill himself and died in 1908.

In Nicodemus where his star first rose, E.P. McCabe is still honored as a favorite son.

Nicodemus is on the Boom! Boom, boom, boom, BOOM!
—The *Western Cyclone*, 1887

Boom times came to Nicodemus, but they took a while to get up to speed. With poor harvests in the early 1880s, many of the settlers lost heart and moved away. By 1884 the township's population had slipped to 239.

But for those steadfast pioneers who stuck with it, patience would be rewarded. The rains returned that year and with them the bumper crops of wheat, rye, barley, and hay.

At last Nicodemus was poised for its biggest—and as it would turn out, the only—economic boom that it would ever know.

Certainly all the pieces for making Nicodemus a social and commercial center were in place. On the townsite were two hotels, two livery stables, a pair of blacksmith shops, four general stores, two drug stores and a variety of specialty shops. Professional services offered included those of a doctor, a law firm, two land offices, and a Bank of Nicodemus where customers could secure their money in a genuine Mosler safe.

For a time, Nicodemus could boast of not one but two weekly newspapers, the *Western Cyclone* founded in 1886 and the competing *Nicodemus Enterprise* appearing a year later. For each you could get a full year's subscription for just $1, paid in advance.

A glimpse of the daily life of the town can be seen in the newspaper columns and advertisements. The ever enterprising Fletcher brothers, Z.T. and T.J., now owned the

Main Street in 1885. The original Baptist church and Foster Williams's general store provide the backdrop for this photograph.

stone-walled St. Francis Hotel and were branching out to farm machinery sales. Zach now was a notary public and an insurance agent as well. Jenny Fletcher had opened a millinery shop carrying a full line of hats, bonnets, plumes, ribbons, thread and buttons, veilings, and lace. "She is," according to her ad, "also prepared to do all kinds of hair dressing."

S. (Samuel) Garland's Nicodemus Land Company offered a full listing of "cheap farms, stock ranches." Stone mason Jonas Moore offered work done to order, while barber C.A. Wilson promised the latest styles. And in an era yet untroubled by links between smoking and health, C.H. Newth's drugstore could proudly advertise "a fine line of cigars."

The two newspapers vied to be the town's leading booster. "Come to Nicodemus to buy goods," the *Western Cyclone* exhorted in striking a blow for local pride. "You can buy anything from a wheelbarrow to a twine binder right here in Nicodemus, and it is your civic duty to patronize home industries. This is what builds up a town."

Nicodemus has no whisky shop; no billiard hall or other gambling hole. Its citizens are a moral, refined people; no drunkenness or rowdyism, no cursing or whooping disturbs the peace.

—The *Western Cyclone*, 1886

The local press also never tired of proclaiming the tranquil nature of their community. Never would Nicodemus be allowed to sink to the level of the lawless cow towns of Western lore. The founders of Nicodemus intended it to be a community of wholesome values, a place where God-fearing people could raise families in safety. And this was one promise they not only kept but exceeded.

Serious crimes were almost unknown in Nicodemus over those first ten years. The near-perfect record was marred only by one reported shooting and two thefts, actual or attempted. There were also three fist fights, one of them said to be between two churchmen who disagreed on Bible interpretations.

In part, perhaps, the general peace could be traced to the Nicodemus Town Company's ban on the sale of liquor in the townsite during the first five years. Those who bought lots signed similar pledges. That sober resolve wavered at one point when a group of citizens petitioned to permit a drug store in Nicodemus to dispense "prescription whiskey." Their petition failed.

"We do not claim sanctification," the *Nicodemus Enterprise* declared in 1887. "But we do claim to be peaceable and even a little more virtuous than some of our howling neighbors."

If you are looking for a safe investment, sure profits, and a home where people are wide awake, take advantage of the cheap rates, pack your grip and steer your bark for Nicodemus. Don't wait, delay will prove dangerous.

—*Nicodemus Cyclone*, 1887

hat the economy of Nicodemus needed most in the 1880s was more people. The decline in the town's population had to be stopped and reversed. More people had to be brought to Nicodemus to build, to buy, and to sell.

So for the second time in ten years, the leaders of Nicodemus launched a campaign to attract new settlers. As before, they exaggerated.

"If there is a paradise on earth,' the *Cyclone* said without blushing, "it certainly is here."

This time the selling of Nicodemus also took on the hard edge of a get-rich-quick scheme. Land values in Nicodemus were rising at such a clip, the *Enterprise* suggested, that those who bought into this paradise on the plains could expect to double their money in a year.

One hitch remained. In the American West of the 1800s, railroads and prosperity went hand in hand. Only railroads could move people and goods on a large enough scale to ensure an economic boom. Nicodemus needed a rail depot of its own.

In 1887 the prospects for a rail line coming to Nicodemus seemed bright. The Missouri Pacific Railroad was planning to extend its tracks beyond Stockton toward Denver. It had a choice of two routes, one that would pass through Nicodemus and another that wouldn't.

Missouri Pacific officials made it known that the choice of routes would depend on the people who lived on the right of way. What they really were asking for was a public subsidy to help pay for the cost of construction—somewhat in the way local governments today offer tax breaks to attract industry to their areas.

How much did the railroad want? The Missouri Pacific wanted $132,000 for the Graham County stretch. Eight towns along the route would give varying amounts, with Nicodemus's share coming to $16,000.

In the spring of 1887, the citizens of Nicodemus voted 92 to 3 to borrow the money by issuing bonds. And when the railroad's surveyors arrived a couple of months later, everyone thought that a Nicodemus rail line was a sure thing.

They were wrong. The Missouri Pacific's track building stalled at Stockton, then stopped.

There were other railroads—two, to be exact.

One was the Santa Fe which also sent surveyors to look Nicodemus over. But then the Santa Fe, too, backed out.

Now all of Nicodemus's hopes lay with the Union Pacific, which was laying tracks along the other side of the South Solomon River. But the other side of the river was where those tracks stayed. More galling still, a temporary rail camp six miles southwest of Nicodemus grew into a rival town called Bogue.

Bypassed by the railroads, Nicodemus's brief boom collapsed. In the final months

The Nicodemus Cyclone *was the town's third—and last—newspaper. It shut down operation in 1888. This issue advertised the upcoming Emancipation Celebration.*

of 1888, every one of the town's white merchants and some of their black colleagues left. Some even dismantled their homes and buildings, piece by piece, and carted them off to new destinations.

Many of the departees resettled in nearby areas. The Bank of Nicodemus, for example, reappeared some weeks later as the Bank of Bogue. Others left the area altogether, some going farther west to Colorado or California.

The two newspapers in Nicodemus merged into one, the *Nicodemus Cyclone*. After repeatedly urging its readers not to panic, the *Cyclone* itself folded after a final issue in November.

No matter how bad it got, we was just so proud of the land.

—R.B. Scruggs in a 1950 interview in the Salina (Kansas) *Journal*

Railroad or no railroad, there were those who did not run—the Bates and Alexanders, the Fletchers, Griffens, Blackmans, Sayers, Switzers, Moores, VanDuvalls, Williams, Wilsons, and a dozen other names still heard in Nicodemus.

They had gone there in the first place to build homes, to farm the land, to raise families, to create a community, to live in freedom. They got on with their lives, and many did quite well.

William Kirtley, the man who brought his personal library with him from Kentucky, did well in Nicodemus. He arrived in 1878 at age twenty-six, homesteaded a quarter section two miles northeast of what is now Bogue, went through three sod houses before putting up a wooden frame house, and lived out the rest of his long life on his own land.

R.B. Scruggs came to Nicodemus when he was seventeen. To supplement his income from farming, Scruggs at one time drove a freight wagon between Nicodemus and Stockton. At other times, he worked as a section hand on the railroad tracks near Salina. By saving his money to put back into land, Scruggs built his holdings over time to 720 acres.

True, the Nicodemus townsite would never again be a thriving hub of commerce. But it never lost its role as the social and cultural center for the African American farmers in the surrounding townships.

Mr. and Mrs. George Sayer and their children Raymond, Calvin, Andrew, and Ethel set down roots in Nicodemus.

Harry Bates in 1895. Harry was two years old and still in skirts, customary fashion for young boys and girls.

An older George Sayer standing in front of the store he ran for years in Nicodemus.

A number of buildings in town survived the flight of businesses from Nicodemus. The two-story stone structure put up by William Green to house his general store, for instance, was recycled and renamed the Masonic Hall. There the Nicodemus chapters of the Masons and its Eastern Star women's auxiliary planned campaigns to help the needy of the community. And there they held weekly socials, highlighted by a big dance party each spring.

At one time or another, organizations such as the American Legion for veterans and 4-H Club for the children played active roles in town. Locally formed groups such as the Priscilla Art Club fostered a sense of community and culture through quilting bees and literary discussions.

By far the most important event in Nicodemus each year was—and still is—the Emancipation Celebration.

The class of 1915 of Fairview School. Most rural schools were contained in one-room schoolhouses and the same teacher taught children of different ages.

This festival originated with the First Grand Independent Benevolent Society of Kansas and Missouri, a self-help group active in Nicodemus in its earliest days. One of the society's traditions was to observe Britain's freeing of West Indian slaves in 1834. And visitors to Nicodemus today are still surprised to learn that the 1834 event—and *not* Abraham Lincoln's Emancipation Proclamation—was the basis of Nicodemus's most enduring institution.

By the 1920s, the Emancipation Celebration had evolved into a big county fair and picnic, so big that it attracted thousands of visitors from miles around.

Sporting events took center stage during the day. There were horse races, boxing matches, and baseball games in which the Nicodemus squad took on teams from all the surrounding communities.

Carnival companies set up rides and games for the children, while many local residents opened food booths offering a sampling of their best home cooking. Outdoor dances and floor shows took up the afternoons and evenings. There were speeches by visiting politicians who could not resist a chance to come by to congratulate all the townspeople.

For years, these "'Demus Day" celebrations were held at Scruggs's Grove, a spot down by the South Solomon River where R.B. Scruggs had planted a grove of cottonwood trees. At night the area was lit by a string of electric bulbs powered by a portable generator. Not until rural electrification finally made it to Nicodemus in the 1950s were the festivities transferred to the townsite itself.

Nowadays, the Emancipation Celebrations are less boisterous and more intimate, less a public festival and more a family gathering. But from the start, they have defined the community and symbolized its values. They still do.

The Dust Bowl years out here were just like a snowstorm every day, only it was brown snow, and it never did melt. It just blew.

—Don Moore

F arming has always been a chancy way to make a living. There are so many things over which the farmer has no control.

There is the weather, of course. It is more than a question of too hot or too cold, too wet or too dry. It is also a matter of too soon or too late. When in the planting cycle did the rains come? Was it a late spring? An early frost? For farmers the answers to such questions spell the difference between a bumper harvest and crop failure.

Crop or livestock prices are also concerns. When demand for farm products is high, the farmer thrives. When it isn't, he could go broke even with a good harvest.

Farming on the Great Plains often seems even chancier than it is in many other places. And in the late 1920s and early 1930s, it was as if everything that could go wrong did go wrong.

First came the Great Depression, when financial markets around the world collapsed. While Wall Street was a long way from the farm belt, the effects of tight money reached the American heartland in a hurry. Farmers could earn little from the sale of their crops, and many went into debt. As the depression lingered, many could not repay their loans and lost their land.

Farmers and their tractors. Many Kansas farmers lost their crops and livelihood when dust storms swept over parts of the Great Plains in the 1930s. Some families abandoned the land totally and sought a new life elsewhere.

On the heels of that disaster came a second blow—a prolonged drought on the southwestern plains. As the land dried to dust, the prairie winds created swirling dust clouds that darkened the skies for hundred of miles.

History books now call those times the Dust Bowl Era. Those who were there and lived through it call it the "Dirty Thirties."

Farmer Don Moore was just a boy then in Nicodemus. "I'd seen the time when you almost choked to death when that dust would come up," he remembered. "It came from the south, from Oklahoma, mostly, I guess. The dust, it wore the animal's teeth out eating feed with so much dirt and grit in it. Grind 'em right down to where they almost couldn't chew the grain after a couple of years. You couldn't raise crops in that dust. We just raised enough feed to take care of the cattle, and that wasn't much."

Nicodemus retiree James Bates was a few years older than Don Moore when those dust clouds blotted out the sun and made days seem like nights:

In those days our houses weren't well sealed, so you'd hang sheets up on the windows and doors. We'd take water and dampen the sheets, so when the dust hit 'em it would stop. You'd get up in the morning, take a scoop shovel and sweep the dirt out.

It blew for days, blew all the crops away. We lost animals and everything that wasn't tied down. When my dad couldn't farm, he was a grader man on the highway crews. My uncle was a bulldozer operator. That's how they made it through, working on highway jobs. They worked all the time to get money to farm.

You see, it wasn't like it is now. It was much harder, but we didn't realize how hard it was. Nobody told us we had it hard.

—Versella Bates

Some basic truths exist about people who work hard. They are usually so busy all their lives that they have little time to feel sorry for themselves.

"See that field over there?" asked Ora Switzer (Sw-EYE-tser), the town matriarch in 1993 at the age of ninety. "I was born in a sod house out in that field. I raised six good kids and a husband out here on this prairie. We farmed forty acres, raised corn, cattle, hogs, chicken. I made my own lard and could can 600 quarts of beets for the winter. We were never hungry a day. Life was fun," she said. "Still is."

Or listen to Don Moore: "We had 160 acres we farmed. As kids, we worked the gardens and stuff and tended the animals and cut the wood and everything else you can think of. We had no electricity, no running water and went to the toilet in outhouses. We raised our own meat, and we raised corn and feed for the cattle. We survived."

"You had to work; there wasn't any choice," said James Bates. "In my family when I came along, we milked a whole bunch of cows and gathered a whole lot of eggs. We milked fifteen, twenty cows a day when I was a boy, twice a day. We separated that milk and separated that cream. When grandma went to town, that cream bought all the groceries for everyone on that place."

Ora Switzer, left, and Ponzetta Garner, right, are life-long residents of Nicodemus.

James Bates's mother, Versella Bates, said the youngsters of Nicodemus knew from an early age what was expected of them:

When it's a matter of surviving, you just never think about inconveniences. We knew our chores. No one had to tell us to go out and pick up chips— wood chips, cow chips. We started a fire in the morning, went out and pumped the water and filled a jug all without being told.

We knew we had to gather the eggs, and get our lessons done before it got too dark because we didn't have but one lamp. You didn't come home and start doing homework at home. You did it before you left school because there were chores at home.

Lord, school was everything to our parents. When I first started, I went to the old school on the townsite. As my family moved around the area, at times I'd walk as far as two miles or take a horse. Some walked four, five miles.

You had to get an education; that's what the old folks believed in. They didn't get it themselves, but they saw to it their children and grand-children would.

*James Bates
and his mother,
Versella Bates.*

We listened to our parents talking about paying the price, about a willingness to sacrifice. Work hard and success will follow, they told us. We listened, and we believed.

—University Administrator Veryl Switzer, in a 1993 interview

Veryl Switzer was the youngest of those "six good kids" reared by Ora Switzer and her late husband, Fred. L. Switzer. Early on, Veryl picked up the nickname "Joe." He does not know how the name originated or why, but he still answers when called by that name.

Otherwise Veryl, or Joe, has forgotten little of his Nicodemus childhood. "For a kid this was a happy place," he said. "My folks were poor. They were always worried about where the next meal would come from, but they didn't let their children know that. My mother was always able to make cornbread, biscuits, gravy, navy beans, black-eyed peas, greens. I didn't know we were living in poverty until I heard that word used many years later."

Sure, there were all those chores: slopping hogs, taking the cattle to pasture, milking cows twice a day. But there were the pleasures of rural life, too. There were horses to ride, fishing down at the river, jackrabbits to hunt. The last two often contributed to the family dinner menu.

Looking back, though, Veryl conceded that there was a downside to rural isolation. Though he grew up on a land where the horizon seems to stretch forever, he found the horizons of his own life oddly confined. "When I was a kid," he remembered, "I really didn't know that there was a someplace else. I had dreamed of going to California because I heard a lot about it, but it had no real significance beyond that. We didn't have television, so I didn't know what California looked like."

His work options and career horizons were similarly restricted. The assumption at the time was that all Nicodemus kids would become farmers or farm wives. "It's hard for anyone in a rural area to get out and go to college, especially if you're black without much money," Veryl said. And there was no one in Nicodemus to serve as professional role models for the kids—"no doctors, no bankers, nothing like that. The lawyer we had here, when I was little, moved on to Colorado."

Veryl himself considered dropping out of school to enlist in the air force. But while attending Bogue Rural High School, he grew close to his principal, a white man, who planted the idea of college in Veryl's head.

Veryl Switzer had several things going for him. First, he was competitive, the kind of person to whom nearly everything is a challenge. "If my cousins could shuck eighty bushels of corn a day, I wanted to do ninety. We competed in everything we did. You never wanted your cousins to beat you."

He was also enterprising. As a youngster, he cleaned chicken coops for neighboring farmers at twenty-five cents per job. He cleaned the Baptist church after services each Sunday for thirty-five cents. By the time he was a teenager, Veryl Switzer was working almost all the time. "In the summers I hired out to neighbors, white neighbors in some cases, and since I was doing a man's work, putting in twelve, fourteen hours a day driving tractors, shocking wheat, I demanded adult pay." (One dollar an hour.)

And he was a natural athlete with size and speed. He starred on a Bogue High football team that went undefeated for two and a half years, walloping opponents by a combined score of 950 points to 52 over that span.

That kind of record attracted notice. Kansas State University offered Veryl a full athletic scholarship, only the second such offer to a black prospect at Kansas State University up to that time.

Veryl Switzer made the most of his chances. He was named an All-American in 1951, selected to the all-Big Seven (later Big Eight) Conference team three times. After graduating from K-State, Switzer wound up in the uniform of the Green Bay Packers. As a running back *and* defensive safety, his finest moment came on a 93-yard kickoff return for a touchdown against the Chicago Bears.

In his time, African Americans were still rare in major college football and the pros. Veryl was the only black player in the Big Seven during his junior year at K-State. And he was the only black on the team during his two seasons with the Packers.

Switzer fulfilled his military obligations as an air force lieutenant, then played three more seasons of pro football in Canada. After that he moved his family to Chicago where he was a physical education teacher in the Chicago public schools. In between school terms, he went back to K-State to earn a master's degree in personnel services and counseling, new skills that he applied in his three years as human relations coordinator in the Chicago school administration.

In 1969 Veryl returned to Kansas and his alma mater, where he took on a variety of assignments and acquired several titles, including associate dean of minority affairs, assistant vice president for student affairs, and associate director of athletics.

Veryl Switzer was one of the first black players to star for the Green Bay Packers. Today, Veryl returns to Nicodemus and often tours the town on his palomino, "Lady."

In a sense, though, Veryl Switzer never left Nicodemus. In the 1960s, he started buying land in his hometown, buying back his heritage, really. Wherever he was, he and his wife, Fern, returned as often as possible to tend to their 800-acre farm.

And something more important: he made himself available to counsel and help the younger generations in Nicodemus, to be a role model that he himself did not have.

"For a long time, high school graduation was the acceptable standard for education in Nicodemus," he said. "I raised the goal one notch. After that, college was a goal we began setting for all our kids.

"It suddenly seemed possible for a farm kid from Nicodemus to make it in the big world."

T he big world outside also had some harsh lessons to teach.

So long as Nicodemus youngsters stayed within their all-black community, they were protected. If they stepped outside of those friendly confines, however, even a short piece down the road, they collided head-on with a painful American reality: racism.

"When you went to high school, that's when you got to see white kids for the first time," James Bates remembered. "Some were good, some were snotty. You'll find that wherever you go. There would be a fight, somebody got whipped, nobody ever got killed, nobody ever got cut, but there was some butt-kicking going on."

It wasn't always that way, said his mother, Versella Bates. "There was a time when I was going to school in Bogue, and the weather was bad. I was accepted in by a white family until the weather cleared up. I slept in their house and ate at their table. Nobody thought anything of it seventy years ago because blacks and whites were all poor, and we needed each other."

Ponzetta Garner recalled a time in the 1920s when she was the only black on the Bogue High girls' basketball team. During a local tournament, the team tried to check into a hotel in Hill City and was met by the manager who told them, "You can't bring that nigger in here."

In that case, all of Ponzetta's teammates agreed, we won't play our game this evening. In that case, said the hotel manager, come on in.

But racial attitudes in and around Graham County hardened with the passing years. Nicodemus and the white communities that surrounded it grew apart. In many nearby white communities, residents boasted that no black would dare remain in their town after sunset

Marvin Switzer is one of Ora Switzer's twenty grandchildren. By the time he was ready for school in the 1960s, the District 1 School in Nicodemus had closed. He and the other Nicodemus kids were bused to Bogue Elementary.

My first day, the kid who sat in front of me was Red Elliott, and I looked at him like he was from outer space. He had real red hair and freckles, and I'd never seen that. He looked at me and said "My dad knows your dad, and your dad's a blackie." I bloodied his nose right there. We grew up to be friends later on.

These swings have hardly been used since the District 1 school closed in 1955.

It was shocking, being around white people for the first time in our lives. The adjustment was hard at first because they didn't like us. I remember people then had to say "Negro." You couldn't say "black" or "nigger."

There was major racism at Bogue High in the late 1960s. There was a lack of black women to date in Graham County because most of us were related, so we started dating white girls. That started a lot of trouble, mostly by parents of the white kids. They'd try to disown their daughters; they compared us to animals.

As long as you packed a football, ran track, dribbled a basketball, and set records, you were okay. But if you crossed [racial lines in dating], that was trouble.

L ike his Uncle Veryl, Marvin Switzer was a fine athlete—all-state in football and basketball. "In 1972 I set the Kansas high school record in the 220-yard dash. The whites liked that because I put Graham County on the map. Don't misunderstand me, there were fine white people back then, but that was [just a few years after] the riots in Los Angeles and Washington and Martin Luther King and all that. It was a confusing time."

At Kansas State University, Marvin Switzer was all-Big Eight defensive back. "I was the second Switzer to attend college; since then there have been a ton of others. All six children in my family graduated college, which is pretty incredible when you consider we were coming from dirt farmers."

Still following in his uncle's footsteps, Marvin turned pro and played a season with the Buffalo Bills and another in the Canadian League. "I encountered racism at that level, too, but by that time I knew how to handle it because of my upbringing in Nicodemus. My grandmother told me, my uncle told me, my parents told me there could never be much growth in you as a person if you don't learn how to handle racism. It sounds trite, but my parents said the white people put their pants on one leg at a time, son."

When we'd go to the restaurants in Hill City, we had to go to the back door and take the food out in a bag," said Charlesetta Bates. "We paid the same price, but we couldn't go inside and eat with the white folks. We could go to the drugstore and have fountain Cokes, that was okay but not the restaurant. It was all mixed up. It made us feel bad, but it was not spoken about much."

"Over in Hill City," her husband James Bates added, "the movie theater had six rows in the balcony for the colored folks. We used to call it the chicken roost. We wouldn't see as good as the white folks downstairs, but we paid the same price. That's just how it was for colored people."

Every now and then, someone would decide that should not be the way it was.

Charlesetta Bates recalled: "One Christmas in the 1940s, we went to see *The Wizard of Oz,* and we just walked in there and sat down in the front and wouldn't move. They wanted us to move. I had small children with me and baby bottles and stuff, hats, and coats, and I wasn't about to move. So I just sat there. They asked again, and I said, 'No,' and just sat there with my son and daughter, and they left us alone. Years later they let us sit downstairs."

Ora Switzer needed a loan back in the 1940s to get the crops planted. She marched into a Hill City bank and was told she needed a mountain of forms filled out, verified, notarized, stamped, stapled, and sworn to. "The heck I do," the indomitable Ora corrected the manager. "You don't make white folks do this. You know me, now gimme the money." He did.

That was then. How about now?

"About fifty percent better," said James Bates, who cited the example of a white couple who ran a Hill City restaurant that did not admit blacks. "But you know," said James, "today they'll stop by and eat ribs with us and never think about or mention the past. It's like the past never happened. They're altogether different people. They learned something, I guess, now that they're older."

James Bates reflected for a moment, then added: "When I had back surgery, I'll be honest with you, none of the colored folks came by. But the white guy farming over there, he said, 'Mr. Bates, anything I can do for you, you let me know. I'll look after the cows for you.' I was in a body cast six months, and he comes here in the winter months, feeds my calves. He has a tractor, he'd blade my driveway off. Another white man said, 'How are you doing, Bates? If you can't get out, I'll send the boys down there for you.'"

"Times have changed," his wife agreed. "God changed things for us. There's more understanding now. Now we have to look to them, and they have to look to us. We're accepted in the county. We've been through the worst.

"Our children today don't have to take what we took," Charlesetta Bates said. "It's a different time, thank God."

Despite a gradual and steady decline, most residents have expressed a growing unwillingness to allow the history of Nicodemus to be forgotten. . . . This intangible sense of history, fueled by over one hundred years of perseverance and rugged determination, can still be detected today.
—United States National Park Service Historian Gregory D. Hendricks in his introduction to *Promised Land on the Solomon: Black Settlement at Nicodemus, Kansas*

Farming in America has changed drastically over the years, and the small family farm has been fighting a losing battle against the giant agricultural operations of today. Young people leave the rural communities as soon as they can, to seek the excitement of the big cities and the better opportunities they offer. The older folks grow older still. Sooner or later, their small farming communities wither, then disappear entirely.

It is the same story all over rural America, especially the farming towns on the Great Plains. Nicodemus is no exception.

James and Charlesetta Bates certainly understood the problem. They left Nicodemus in 1957. "There was nothing for us to do here, and when we were younger, getting out seemed important," said James. "You couldn't better yourself here. You get that hunger. We left with the idea of making a better living. I had only a few pennies and

James and Charlesetta Bates enjoy retirement on their 40-acre farm just north of town.

six kids to feed when I went to the California country," added James, who drove a truck for the City of Pasadena. "Never took a day off," he said proudly. Charlesetta Bates worked as a cook.

Like many others from Nicodemus, however, the Bates moved away from their hometown without ever really leaving. They always regarded their absence as temporary. They always knew that, one day, they would go home.

Which was what happened when James retired in 1981. They went back to Nicodemus, paid $12,000 from their savings for forty acres just a long stone's throw north of the townsite and built a small house. There, James sits on his front porch and reflects on a life well spent:

> Hard work paid off for me and my family. All of my children did pretty good. I taught them to get an education, get a good job, and stay out of trouble. One son is an over the road trucker, a daughter works at Cal State, and another for some big bank. Now you take the grandchildren coming up, they have it too, the desire to do better. One of my granddaughters wants to become an architect. I got a grandson attending Howard University. I got one at Kansas State.

Along with their successes, James and Charlesetta Bates made sure their children never forgot their roots. "I moved with my parents to Pasadena when I was four," said Angela Bates, their youngest. "But I spend every summer back in Nicodemus because my parents taught me that no matter where we lived, Nicodemus is our home."

After her graduation from Emporia (Kansas) State University, Angela Bates worked as an interior decorator in Denver and Washington, D.C., before going back to Nicodemus to stay in 1990. "I came back to be close to my family," she said, "and to be close to the land. There's an affinity to the land even if you don't farm. When you live in a rural area like western Kansas, you know you are a part of this planet, Earth, something

Angela Bates visits the grave of her great-great grandfather, original settler Perry Bates.

larger than yourself. That love of the land and the open skies, coupled with the strong heritage of Nicodemus, compelled me to return."

The same mystical sense of place is what drove Veryl and Fern Switzer to make the 400-mile round trip from K-State in Manhattan, Kansas, back to Nicodemus on so many weekends. "I kept buying land back here because I wanted to remain a part of this place," Veryl said. "This land has meaning for me. It's around me and in me; it still speaks back to me."

Some years ago, Veryl Switzer bought the house in the townsite in which he was born—Zach Fletcher's old St. Francis Hotel with its three-foot thick limestone walls, built in 1881. "I like having the thread that runs back to my ancestors," he explained. "When you think about that, you really appreciate what they did for us, what it took for them to survive in this harsh land.

"This place to us is like a living family museum," Veryl Switzer said. "You can still feel it and touch it. At least I can."

Nicodemus isn't just for Nicodemus. It's for the rest of the world, too.
—Nicodemus-born writer Debra Alexander-O'Hara
in the Wichita *Eagle*, 1993

Outsiders have given Nicodemus up for dead many times before—when its post office was closed and when its one-room schoolhouse was abandoned in the 1950s; when Ernestine's Barbecue, the last business in town, shut down in the 1980s.

But defying the odds is a long-standing Nicodemus tradition.

For the residents of Nicodemus and their far-flung descendants, the desire to keep their town alive goes beyond the preservation of treasured memories. They know that in its stories of the warmth and support of families, of an unshakable faith in God and in the value of hard work, Nicodemus is as much an idea as it is a place.

Or as the Nicodemus Historical Society's President Angela Bates put it: "It's the spiritual experience of Nicodemus, a feeling, emotion. The solutions to society's problems can be found here in family, friendships, hard work, and a sense of community—the things that matter in life. It's all here on the plains of western Kansas.

"So we think Nicodemus needs to be preserved and proclaimed for its historic significance," she said, "not for blacks alone, but for all Americans."

A Homecoming is a time to recall the past, celebrate the present, and renew ties to family and friends.

Happily, a plan was well underway to do just that. The new idea was to convert Nicodemus from a National Historical Landmark to a National Historical Site, a rise in status that would place it more firmly within the U.S. Park System. This, in turn, would bring a higher level of federal support in preserving Nicodemus as an American cultural and educational resource.

Initially, this plan called for the repair and restoration of four historic buildings: the District 1 schoolhouse, the St. Francis Hotel, and the old First Baptist and African Methodist churches. The National Park Service would manage the historical sites with the full participation of the local community.

Start-up costs were expected to come in at around $2.7 million, and these funds must be approved by the U.S. Congress. Indeed, a Nicodemus bill was scheduled to be introduced by Senator Robert Dole of Kansas in the early months of 1995.

The long-term hope is that a rebuilt Nicodemus will draw growing numbers of visitors there to be inspired and instructed by the story of this little prairie town that would not quit. To this day, no one in Nicodemus doubts that the survival of their community still rests on the kind of determination and hard work displayed by their pioneering forebears more than 100 years ago.

"Nicodemus has always produced successful people," Marvin Switzer said. "I think it's because as kids we all sat around and listened to the old people talk about how they never gave up.

"Not giving up," he said, "is part of our heritage."

1854   Kansas-Nebraska Act. Congress formally creates the frontier territories of Kansas and Nebraska. The issue of slavery in the new territories is to be decided by settlers there.

1861   Kansas enters the Union as a free state.

1861   American Civil War begins.

1862   Homestead Act is passed by Congress. Act grants free parcels of public land to settlers after five years' residence.

1863   President Abraham Lincoln issues the Emancipation Proclamation freeing all slaves in areas still in rebellion against the United States.

1865   Civil War ends in Union victory.

1865   The Thirteenth Amendment ends slavery.

1865-77   Reconstruction Era.

1869   Union Pacific and Central Pacific Railroads meet in Utah and link east-west rails.

1877	First black colonists reach the new town of Nicodemus.
1878	First Emancipation Celebration is held in Nicodemus. Post Office is established.
1879	School District No. 1 is established in Nicodemus, the first in Graham County.
1879-80	Thousands of "Exodusters" from the South pour into Kansas.
1885-88	Nicodemus enjoys a brief boom period.
1889	Railroad lines bypass Nicodemus and send town into extended decline.
1929	The Great Depression begins.
1934-37	The Dust Bowl era on the Great Plains.
1953	Nicodemus Post Office is closed.
1955	The last of the one-room school houses in Nicodemus shuts down.
1976	Nicodemus is designated a National Historical Landmark historical district by the United States Secretary of the Interior.
1993	National Park Service completes a study on suitability of Nicodemus as a National Historical Site within the park system.

Crockett, Norman L. *The Black Towns*. Lawrence, KS: Regents Press of Kansas, 1979.
An encompassing look at the racial, political, and economic factors underlying the founding of all-black towns in Oklahoma (Boley, Langston City, Clearview), Mississippi (Mound Bayou), and Kansas (Nicodemus).

Frazier, Ian. *Great Plains*. New York: Penguin Books, 1989. A delightful account of the author's travels through the Great Plains, including a personal visit to Nicodemus.

Hamilton, Kenneth Marvin. *Black Towns and Profit*. Urbana and Chicago, IL: University of Illinois Press, 1991. Nicodemus and four other communities (Boley, Langston City, and Mound Bayou plus Allensworth, California) that began as all-black towns are examined in this detailed study. The author argues with some success that economic motives out weighed racial factors in their founding.

Katz, William Loren. *The Black West,* 3rd Revised Edition. Seattle, WA: Open Hand Publishing, Inc., 1987. Despite scant mention of Nicodemus, this work provides a useful overview of the entire black experience throughout the frontier West.

Miner, Craig. *West of Wichita*. Lawrence, KS: University Press of Kansas, 1986.
A moving, wonderfully written description of pioneering life on the Kansas High Plains during the second half of the nineteenth century.

Schwendemann, Glen. *Nicodemus: Negro Haven on the Solomon*. Topeka, KS: State of Kansas Commission on Civil Rights, 1971. A reprint from the *Kansas Historical Quarterly*, this brief article remains one of the best accounts of the early days of Nicodemus.

United States Department of the Interior, National Park Service. *Promised Land on the Solomon: Black Settlement at Nicodemus, Kansas*, 1983. This joint project of the National Park Service, the Kansas State Historical Society, Kansas State University, and Entourage, Inc. is the most complete and thoroughly documented study of Nicodemus ever undertaken. The book is no longer available from the United States Government Printing Office, but the Nicodemus Historical Society (R.R. #2, Box 131, Nicodemus, KS 67625) planned a reprinting.

ACKNOWLEDGMENTS

The authors wish to thank the many individuals who gave generously of their expertise and time in assisting us in the preparation of this book.

We are especially grateful to Angela Bates, president of the Nicodemus Historical Society, and the many residents of Nicodemus who clarified the records and shared their personal reminiscences with us; to the unfailingly courteous and endlessly patient group at Kansas State University in Manhattan—Pat Patton, at the University Archives, Huber Self, professor emeritus of geography, and Veryl Switzer, associate director of athletics; to Phyllis Schmidt, assistant librarian at Ft. Hays (Kansas) State University for making several unpublished Nicodemus manuscripts available to us; to Deborah Dandridge, archivist of the Kansas Collection at the University of Kansas in Lawrence for her help in picture research and to the staffs of the Kansas State Historical Society in Topeka and the Schomburg Center for Research in Black Culture of the New York City Public Library for making their resources available to us.

Special thanks also to Mrs. Henry A. Humphrey of Wichita for her personal knowledge of Kansas history and lore; to John Nickerson, Joan Traub, and Denise Crawford for reading the manuscript and making numerous useful comments; to Barbara Russiello for her help and encouragement; and to Jay Grayson for his assistance in photographic printing and to our editor, Adriane Ruggiero at Julian Messner, who backed our project from the start and shepherded it to print.

If errors of fact or interpretation have crept into our manuscript even with this formidable support, the fault lies entirely with the authors.

INDEX

Note: Page references to illustrations
    are in *italics*.

alcohol, 55
Alexander-O'Hara, Debra, 87
Athearn, Robert G., 20

Bates, Angela, 8, 84, *85,* 87, 94
Bates, Charlesetta, 80,81-84, *83*
Bates, Henry, *61*
Bates, James, 67, 68, 70, *71,* 76,
    81-84, *83*
Bates, Perry, *85*
Bates, Versella, 39, 68, 70, *71,* 77
Belleau, William J., 34
Benton, Thomas Hart,"Ploughing It
    Under," *22*
Bogue (Kansas), *57, 59,* 73, 74, 77, 79
Brown, John, 20, 23-24, *24*
Buffalo Bills, 80
buffalo bones, 40
buffalo chips, 38

Cherokee County (Kansas), 25
Chicago (Illinois), 50, 51, 74
Constitution, amendments to, 20
Curry, John Steuart, painting by, *24*

droughts, 19, 67
dugouts, 7, 36-39, 42, 47
dust storms, 65-67

Elliott, Red, 77
Ellis (Kansas), 7, 9, 35, 36, 47

Emancipation Celebration
    (Homecoming), 13-14, *13, 58,*
    62-64, *88*
Exodusters, 25-27, *26*

farming
    dry-land, 19
    in early Nicodemus, 39-40, 42
    hard life of, 68-70
    in 1930s, 65-67, *66*
    ranchers and, 48
    in recent years, 82
    sharecropping, 21, *22*
Fifteenth Amendment, 20
First Baptist Church (Nicodemus), 12, *12*
First Grand Independent Benevolent
    Society of Kansas and Missouri, 63
fleas, 45
Fletcher, Jenny, 35, 47, 54
Fletcher, Thomas J., 35, 52
Fletcher, Zach T., 35, 47, 52-53, 86
Fourteenth Amendment, 20
Freedman's Bureau, 21

Garland, Samuel, 54
Garner, Ponzetta, *69,* 77
Georgetown (Kentucky), 5-6, 39
Graham County (Kansas), 9, 33, 34, 47,
    50, *57,* 77, 79
"Great American Desert," 16, 19
Great Depression, 65
Great Plains, 8, 16-19, *17,* 34, 82
Green, William, 49
Green Bay Packers, 74, *75*

Hall, Abraham T., 50
Harpers Ferry (West Virginia), 23
Hendricks, Gregory D., 82
Hickman, Rev. Daniel, *5,* 6, 46, 50
Hickman, Willianna, 5-8, 38
Hill, William R., 5-6, 27-29, *28,* 33-36
Hill City (Kansas), 28, 29, 77, 80, 81
Homecoming. *See* Emancipation
    Celebration
homesteading, 6, 18-19, 27
horses, 34, 39, 42, 72

insects, 45

Jim Crow laws, 21

Kansas
    first black Auditor in, 50
    as free state, 23
    map of, *10*
    painting in State Capitol, *24*
Kansas City *Star,* 41
"Kansas itch," 45
Kansas State University, 74, 79, 84,
    86, 94
Kirtley, William, 46, 60
Ku Klux Klan, 21

labor unions, 21
Langston City (Oklahoma), 51
Lawrence (Kansas), 23
Lee, Rev. Silas M., 46
Lexington (Kentucky), 36
Liberty (Oklahoma), 51

limestone, 43, *44*, 86
Long, Stephen H., 16

McCabe, Edward P., 50-51, *51*
Manifest Destiny, 19
Masonic Hall (Nicodemus), 62
Michigan State Fair, 41
Missouri Pacific Railroad, 57
Moore, Don, 35, 65, 67
Moore, Jonas, 54
Mormons, 16
Mount Olive (Kansas), 46

Newth, C.H., 49, 54
Nicodemus (Kansas)
    advertising for, 29-34, *33*, 56
    building up of, 42-47, *44*
    businesses in, 47, 49, 52-54, *53*, 62,
      62, 87
    chronology of, 90-91
    churches in, 12, *12*, 46, *53*
    decline of, 60, 82, 87, 91
    description and views of, *4*, 9-11, *11*
    early days in, 7, 26-31, 35-42
    early fees in, 31
    education in, 46-47, *63*, 70, 77,
      78, 87
    first baby in, 37
    founding of, 6
    location of, 9-11
    map of, 32
    medical care in, 49
    morals in, 55
    as National Historical Landmark,
      11, 89, 91
    population of, 12, 39, 49-50, 52

post office at, 47, 91
social organizations in, 62
street names in, 31
Township Hall, 13-14, *13*
Nicodemus (legendary figure), 29
Nicodemus Cyclone, 56, *58, 59*
Nicodemus Enterprise, 52, 55
Nicodemus Historical Society, 8, 87

Oklahoma, all-black towns in, 51
"Old Pap" Singleton, 24-25, 27
Osage Indians, 37

paintings, *22, 24*
Perfax, Miranda, *14*
Pike, Zebulon, 16
pioneers, black, 6-7, 20, 23, 25-26,
    34-40
"Ploughing It Under" (Benton), *22*
prairies, *17*, 19

Quick, Angela, *14*

racism, 76-80
railroads, 18-19, *56-57*
rattlesnakes, 45
Reconstruction, 20-21
Roundtree, Rev. Simon P., 29, 33,
    35, 41

St. John, John Pierce, 25, 50
Salina (Kansas) *Journal*, 60
Santa Fe railroad, 57
Sayer, George, *61, 62*
Sayers, W.L., 34
Scruggs, R.B., 60, 64

Singleton, Benjamin "Pap," 24-25, 27
slavery, 5, 20-21, 25, 29, 45
    Brown's revolt against, 23-24
    in West Indies, 63-64
Smith, W.H., 27-29, 33
sod houses, 43-45, 60
Solomon River, 29, 33
South Solomon River, 64
Stockton (Kansas), 36, 57, 60
Switzer, Fern, 76, 86
Switzer, Fred. L., 72
Switzer, Marvin, 15, 77, 79-80, 89
Switzer, Ora, 68, *69*, 72, 77, 81
Switzer, Veryl "Joe," 72-76, *75*, 86, 94

Thirteenth Amendment, 20
Topeka (Kansas), *24, 26*, 35, 50
Topeka (Kansas) *Daily Capital*, 7
tornadoes, 19
town companies, 27-29
Turner, Frederick Jackson, 18

Union Pacific Railroad, 57
Utah, 16

"Wake Nicodemus" (song), 29-30
Western Cyclone, 52, 54-56
Wichita *Eagle*, 87
wild fires, 19, 45, 48
Williams, Charles, 37
Williams, Emily, 37
Williams, Foster, *53*
Williams, Henry, 37, *38*
Wilson, C.A., 54
Wilson, Samuel G., 49
wolves, 35